A TRUE BOOK™

AF511568

CLICK, SWIPE, LEARN: SKILLS FOR THE DIGITAL WORLD

Cody Crane

Children's Press®
An imprint of Scholastic Inc.

Thank you to our expert content consultant:
Heidi Julien, Ph.D.
Professor and UB Exceptional Scholar – Sustained Achievement
Department of Information Science
University at Buffalo SUNY

and our educational consultant:
Jackie Fego
Science Liaison
C.V. Starr Intermediate School
Brewster, NY

Copyright © 2026 by Scholastic Inc.

All rights reserved. Published by Children's Press, an imprint of Scholastic Inc., *Publishers since 1920*. SCHOLASTIC, CHILDREN'S PRESS, A TRUE BOOK™, and associated logos are trademarks and/or registered trademarks of Scholastic Inc.

The publisher does not have any control over and does not assume any responsibility for author or third-party websites or their content.

No part of this publication may be reproduced, stored in a retrieval system, or transmitted in any form or by any means, electronic, mechanical, photocopying, recording, or otherwise, or used to train any artificial intelligence technologies, without written permission of the publisher. For information regarding permission, write to Scholastic Inc., Attention: Permissions Department, 557 Broadway, New York, NY 10012.

Library of Congress Cataloging-in-Publication Data available

ISBN 978-93-5954-946-0

Printed in India at Shiv Shakti Printing and Trading Co., Haryana
This reprint edition: November 2025

Design by Kathleen Petelinsek
Series produced by Spooky Cheetah Press

Find the Truth!

Everything you are about to read is true ***except*** for one of the sentences on this page.

Which one is **TRUE**?

TRUE or FALSE It is never okay to reuse content others have posted online.

TRUE or FALSE Many apps have features to keep people using them as long as possible.

Find the answers in this book.

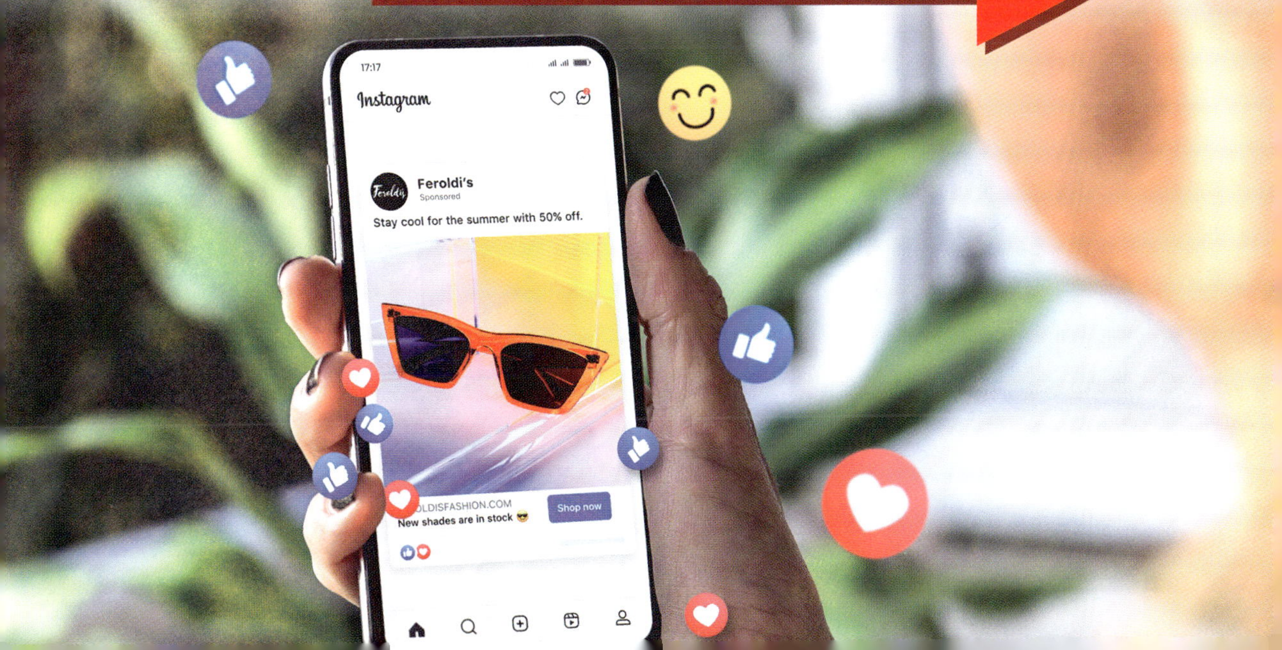

What's in This Book?

Clickbait is content that is meant to grab your attention.

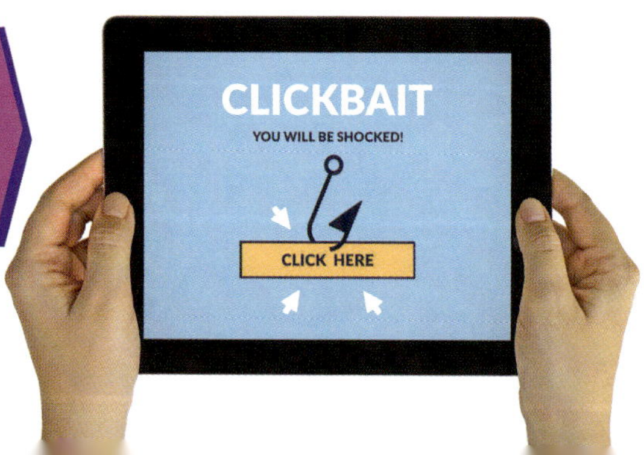

Seeing is not always believing. Photos can be faked.

With new technologies, creating fake content is easier than ever before.

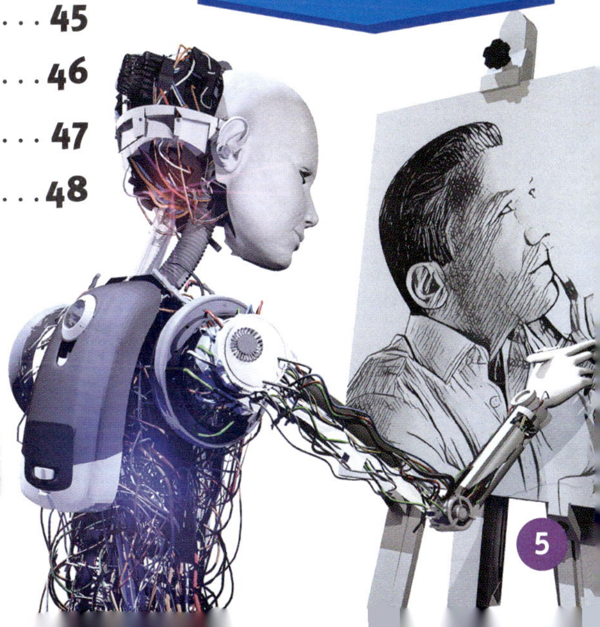

Look for this symbol throughout the book. Pause and reflect to answer the questions.

INTRODUCTION

People all over the world rely on the internet. That includes kids like you! People **go online** for school, for work, to talk with friends and family, and for fun! The internet is a big part of our daily lives, so it is important to know how to use it. To do that, you need to know **how to be safe online**. You also need to have good **digital literacy** skills. These skills will help you successfully evaluate, find, and share information online. In this book, you will learn how to **spot false information**, **find websites** you can trust, and use the **internet responsibly**. Get ready to learn the skills you need for the digital world!

Learn more about this by reading the book *Surf Smart: Staying Safe Online* in this series.

A very important skill is knowing when to put away the device.

Made-up information is also known as *misinformation.*

What is something you have seen online that might not have been true?

CHAPTER

1

Spotting Fake Information

You search online for the best toys for your new puppy. One search result surprises you. It says, "Squeaky balls are no fun. Dogs actually hate playing fetch!" Wait a minute. Is that true? The internet contains a lot of information. Sadly, not all of it is reliable. Sometimes, you might not get the whole truth. Other times, what you read is totally made-up! Just knowing *that* is the first step to spotting fake information.

The Spread of False Ideas

There are many reasons people might post something that is not true online. It might be a joke, like an April Fools' Day prank, that is meant to be funny. But most times, people post fake rumors or lies about a topic to try to change other people's opinion about something. Because people share information online, these false ideas can spread quickly.

Companies often announce fake products online as April Fools' Day jokes. In 2024, 7-Eleven offered hot dog–flavored water!

Misinformation is meant to mislead people.

"Deepfakes" are images, videos, or audio files of people created by AI that look or sound like they are real.

The Rise of AI

Artificial intelligence, or AI, has made creating fake online **content** even easier. This technology can quickly generate images, songs, videos, and texts that seem like they were made by a human. Often, the AI content looks or sounds so realistic it can be hard to tell it's fake. It can even show real people, like a country's president, doing or saying something that never actually happened. That can fool many people.

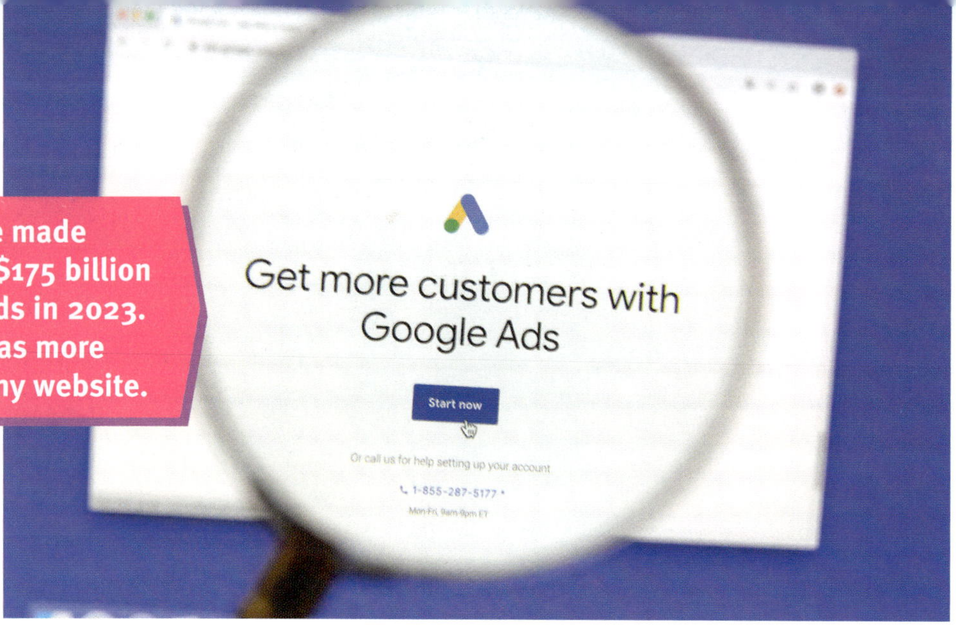

Google made about $175 billion from ads in 2023. That was more than any website.

False Text

Most websites include ads. That is how they make money. But these ads can be misleading. Companies might make false claims about products to get you to click and buy. For example, they might say their product can make you stronger or smarter. Companies also sponsor, or pay for, content that features their products. Unless you pay close attention, you might not even realize that a post or video is really an ad in disguise.

Should You Click?

Online content creators want other people to visit their accounts. More followers means they will get more money from advertisers. So they often use posts known as "clickbait" to draw people in. These links use catchy headlines or surprising images to get you to click. But they do not provide the information they promise. Here are some examples.

What You Might See	Why It Might Be Misleading
"Bigfoot Caught on Camera!"	It seems unbelievable.
"School Playgrounds Too Dangerous for Students!!!"	It is meant to be shocking.
"Famous Movie Star Spotted on Shopping Spree"	It features gossip about a celebrity or another popular topic.
"10 Ways to Get Out of Doing Homework"	It promises something too good to be true.

The term *clickbait* combines *click*, referring to using a computer mouse, and *bait*, which is something used to lure someone.

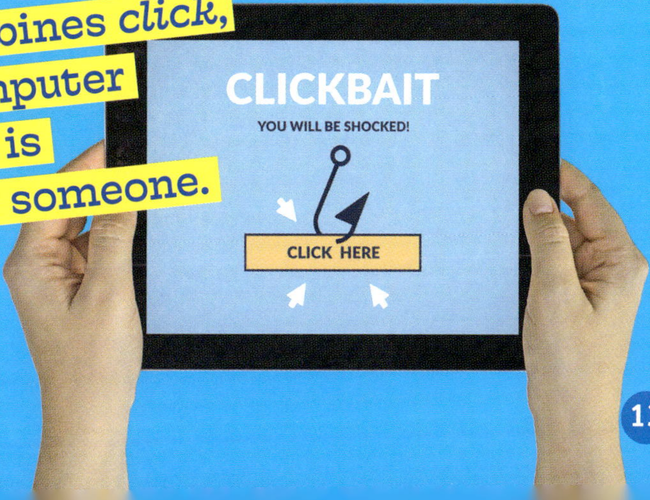

False Images

In real life, seeing is believing. That is not always the case online. People can use digital tools to edit, or change, how images look. They might do this to be creative. But they also might be trying to make you believe something that is not true or get you to click. You should doubt any image online that seems impossible or too perfect. Here are two examples.

A surprising image like this might be used as clickbait.

Unicorn seen for the first time!

A person might post an image like this as a hoax to trick others.

This drink took my game to the next level!

Which of these fake images would you have believed?

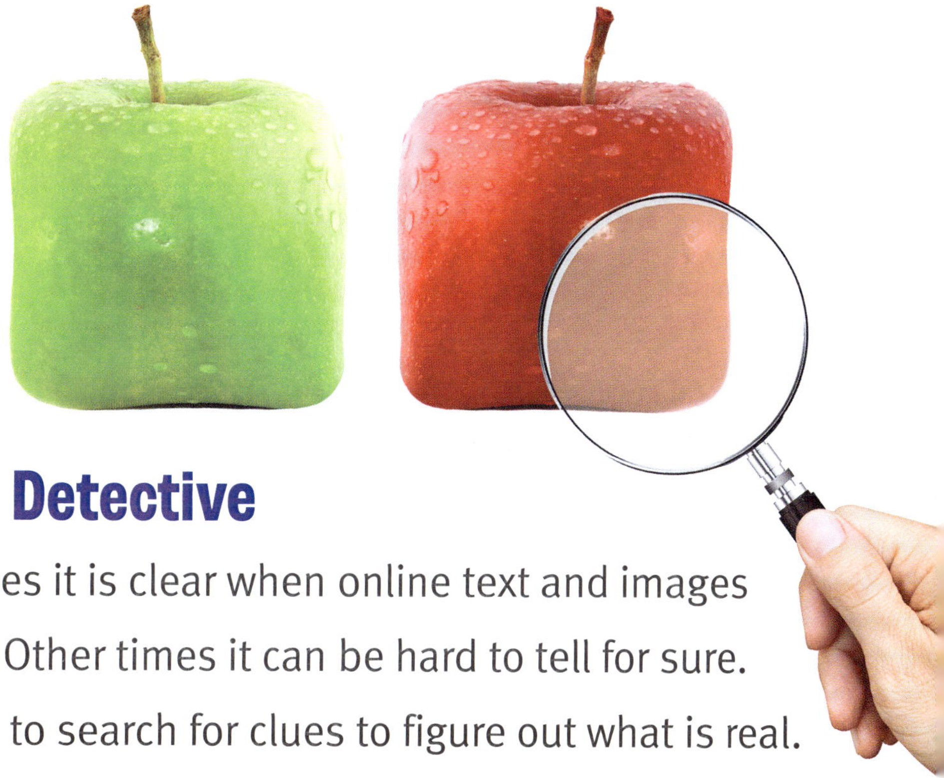

These photos are not real!

Digital Detective

Sometimes it is clear when online text and images are fake. Other times it can be hard to tell for sure. You have to search for clues to figure out what is real.

Ask Yourself . . .	It Might Be Fake If . . .
Where did I find this?	It was posted on a social media site or shared by someone.
Why did someone post this?	The person got paid or tried to sell you something when you visited their site.
Did I get the full story?	It seemed like it was trying to convince you of something.
Did anything about this seem strange?	It looked or sounded too perfect, showed something that is impossible, or seemed slightly off.

There are more than one billion websites online. Not all of them contain reliable sources of information.

Finding reliable information online can be hard! But it is a skill you can learn!

CHAPTER

2

Finding the Real Facts

You are assigned a class project to research recent hurricanes. What is the first thing you do? You go online—where you find lots of information about these huge storms. But now you know that not everything online is accurate. You need to sift through all these sources to find information that is **credible**. This chapter will show you how to make sure the facts you find online are the real deal.

Searching Online

Some people find information online using a **search engine**. The results are ordered from top to bottom based on how best they relate to what you searched for. But be careful: Some browsers show ads as top results. Many browsers also show AI-created answers first. These answers, as well as those generated by AI tools like ChatGPT, can include incorrect or even made-up information.

Google is the most popular search engine in the world. Bing and Yahoo! come next.

Wikipedia contains entries in more than 300 languages.

Is Wikipedia a Credible Source?

It is likely you have come across a website called Wikipedia. It is a free online encyclopedia anyone can update. It contains information on just about everything. But since anyone can make changes to the site, this can affect how credible its information is. Wikipedia is a good place to start learning about a topic. But you should always verify that the information you find on the site is factual, or trustworthy. Keep reading to learn how.

Credibility Check

When you visit a website, you should make sure it is a trustworthy place to find information. Here is what to look for.

- ✔ **Check the source.** The most credible sources online are well-known news sites and those run by universities. Website endings tell you whether it belongs to a school (.edu), the government (.gov), or a business (.com).
- ✔ **Check your reaction.** If the information did not make sense or was hard to believe, it is likely not a credible source.
- ✔ **Check other places.** Look for the same information on other credible sites. They should confirm or support what you read.

Timeline of Information Online

1980
The Columbus Dispatch **becomes the first online newspaper.**

1994
The US Library of Congress, the world's largest library, gives people online access to its collections.

2001
Wikipedia is launched. It is a free online encyclopedia anyone can update.

Where Do You Get Your News?

In the past, people kept up with current events by reading the newspaper, watching TV, or listening to the radio. But today, most people get their news online—especially from social media. That has become a problem because anyone can post made-up information about real topics online. They can then pass off this information as "news." So it is best to get your news only from established news sites.

"Fake news" is used to describe false information about real topics created to fool people.

2016
Some social media networks begin to flag fake news shared on their sites.

2017
The first International Fact-Checking Day is created to fight online misinformation.

2020
Fake AI-created images and videos of real people begin to appear online.

2024
Google begins to include AI summaries for searches.

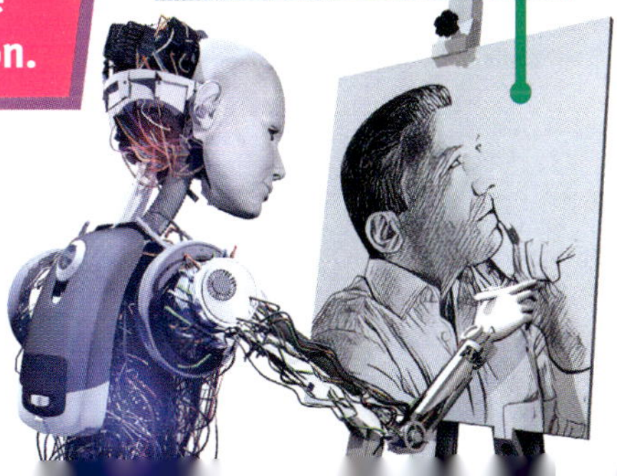

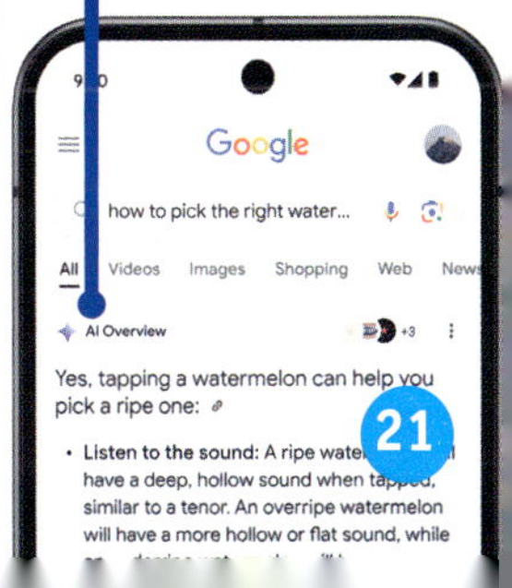

Fact-Check

If a news article is from a trusted site, it should have the following features.

Many U.S. newspapers have online news sites. However, most news sites found online contain fake information.

What to Check For

1. The website is one you know and trust.
2. Photos say where they came from, so you know they are real.
3. The headline matches what the article is about.
4. The author is listed, so you can search to find out more about them.
5. The text includes quotes and sources that show the reporter researched to get the facts.

There are ways to tell a fake news site from a real one.

Editorials and opinion pieces give the opinion of a person familiar with a certain topic.

One-Sided Story?

Usually, credible news articles give all the facts related to a story. But sometimes, even trusted news sites post articles that give only one point of view. These articles are called editorials. You can spot them because they are labeled “Editorial” or “Opinion” near the headline. It is important to be aware that these articles can contain **bias**.

Why do you think newspapers publish editorials if they contain bias?

The BIG Truth

Are YOU Biased?

You read online that people's favorite dessert is chocolate cake. You think that must be right because chocolate cake is your favorite dessert too. Not so fast! That could just be your **personal bias** talking. Bias is a preference for or against something. **Everyone is biased** in some way. But bias can lead us to **believe things** that are **not true**.

How does bias work?

Our brains receive tons of information each day. They have to decide what is important and what is not. To do that, our brains latch on to ideas that seem to fit with what we already think we know. This confirms what we already believe—like, for example, that chocolate cake is the best.

How can bias affect you?

Bias can affect how we see others and the world around us. Sometimes, that can be in negative ways. Bias might make you think a person is strange if they like ice cream better than cake.

Does the internet make bias worse?

Websites and apps collect data on what you search for and view online. They then show you more of the same type of content. That can strengthen your biases. You might start to see more posts about chocolate cake, which makes you even more sure it is everyone's favorite.

How can you combat bias?

Be open to new ideas and views that are different from your own. Celebrate people's differences. Find out more about a topic before you jump to conclusions. For example, combat bias by learning about people's favorite desserts around the world.

Confirmation bias is the idea that we favor information that matches our own beliefs and opinions.

Movies, TV shows, and music are the most-often copied and shared types of online content.

Selling another person's artwork without permission is stealing.

CHAPTER

3

Giving Credit

You post a cool drawing of a dinosaur you made online. Then you start to see your picture everywhere on the internet. People are sharing it with one another. But that is not all. You start seeing websites selling T-shirts and posters with exact copies of YOUR dinosaur drawing. If you think that is unfair, you are right. It may even be illegal. There are rules about when people can and cannot use things others have created.

The first copyright law was created in 1710 in England to protect publishers and authors.

Who Owns It?

The copyright law says that when a person creates any kind of visual or written work, it is their property. It belongs to them. The work could be a photo, a poem, an essay, a song, a video, or a piece of art. They are all protected by **copyright**. This law allows only the person who created a work to decide how it is used. In most cases, anyone else would need permission from its creator. And they might need to pay to use it. However, there are some exceptions . . .

Students Are Protected

You might have used someone else's work you found online for a school project. If so, do not worry. You did not do anything illegal. Copyright allows teachers and students to use materials from the internet for educational purposes. This is called **fair use**. The law says this is okay because many people are being helped by learning from the content.

Copyrights expire. That happened to the original Mickey Mouse, which was created in 1928. Now anyone can use that character.

Even in the case of fair use, you cannot reproduce another person's work in its entirety.

Fair Use Beyond School

There are other cases when you can use something without the original creator's permission. That is the case only if at least one of the following is true.

- You are not using the original work to make money.
- The work is part of a news story or historical documentary.
- You do not lower the value of the original work.
- You use only a small portion of the original work.
- You turn the work into something new and use it for a different purpose than the original.
- You are making a joke, providing an opinion, or commenting on the work.

Mona Lisa, by Leonardo da Vinci

Mona Lisa **is in the public domain—this means anyone can use it. That is because the artist died more than 500 years ago.**

A site might ask you to remove content or disable your account if you post copyrighted material that does not meet fair use.

AI and Fair Use

Some AI tools can have realistic conversations. Others can create images that look like they were made by an actual artist. Scientists train AI to mimic humans by having them study thousands of works people have created that were found online. That has sparked a big debate. AI companies say these applications are protected by fair use because they are using only small portions of the original works, and the resulting works are used for a different purpose than originally intended. But authors and artists say AI should not be using their copyrighted material without their consent.

Does using copyrighted materials to train AI sound like fair use to you?

There are programs that can help teachers tell when work is not your own.

Is It Stealing?

While researching a report for school, you find a paragraph online. It perfectly describes your paper's topic. You copy the text in your own handwriting. Then you turn it in. Bad idea! That is **plagiarism**. Putting your name to someone else's words is stealing. The same goes for using AI to write your report because you are not using your own words.

Giving Credit

If you use someone else's words, ideas, or images for schoolwork, you should give them credit. You do this by **citing**, or saying, where the material originally came from. Include information about who made the work, its title, and where you found it. Citing shows that you are using credible information.

What might be some consequences of not giving credit to original sources?

Citing respects the person who created the original material.

Spending time online can be fun, but so is spending time with other people!

CHAPTER 4

Healthy Online Habits

You have been scrolling through websites since you got home from school. Have you been staring at a screen for too long? If you lost track of how much time you have been online, the answer is "Yes!" Using devices should not keep you from doing more important things, like exercising, doing homework, being outdoors, and spending time with others.

Do you feel like you spend too much, too little, or just the right amount of time online each day?

Stuck to Your Screen

Online sites and apps want you to stay glued to your screen. That is because they can show you ads, which is how they make money. They often have built-in features to keep you engaged. That includes auto-play videos, endless scrolling, and notifications. There is another reason it is hard to put down devices. Every time you score in a game or someone "likes" something you've posted, your brain gets a boost of feel-good chemicals like serotonin.

Take a break from your screen if you are using a device just because you are bored.

A good night's sleep is important for concentration.

Light given off by screens can trick your brain into thinking it is daytime and make it hard to fall asleep.

Lack of Sleep

Yawn! You did not get enough sleep last night, and you have a big test today. Maybe you should not have stayed up so late using a device. That is a common problem for many kids. Children ages 6 to 12 need 9 to 12 hours of sleep per night. But many kids do not get enough sleep. To get the sleep you need, you should stop using devices at least one hour before bedtime.

Put Your Phone Down

Try not to get in the habit of using your device mindlessly.

Kids ages 11 to 17 with phones get about 240 notifications a day!

Better Choices

Screen time should be a positive experience that helps you in some way. Here is how to make sure you benefit from being online.

- **Do Not Get Distracted:** Turn off features, like notifications, meant to keep you on your device.
- **Have a Purpose:** Use devices for a reason, like to solve a problem, interact with others, or create something new.
- **Limit Screen Time:** Only use devices for a set time so you free up time to do other things.
- **Be Respectful:** Devices are not more important than people. If someone is speaking to you, put down your device.

Leveled-Up Online Skills!

You have learned a lot to improve your digital literacy skills. You know that information on the internet is not always trustworthy. And you can sort online facts from fiction. You also know when and how you can reuse online works created by other people. Most important, you have learned to build better habits to balance time online and off. Now you are ready for the digital world!

Good digital habits can make screen time fun instead of stressful.

How do you feel about your digital literacy skills after reading this book?

Fake News Finder

To start this activity, cover page 41 with a sheet of paper or a large book. Done? Now, please continue reading! Fake news sites can often look very similar to real online news articles. But if you examine them closely, you will notice some things are off. Can you find the six things that tell you this news article is fake? If you need help, revisit Chapter 2. Then check the answers on page 41.

https://wownewsnow.net

All Bookmarks

WOW NEWS NOW

May 4, 2018

ALIENS FOUND ON EARTH!

Reports of real-life aliens living among us.

By Staff Reporter

Want to see real-life aliens? Here is a list of places to travel to see signs that aliens have visited our planet, sponsored by travel.com.

Aliens might have landed on Earth in 1947. A spaceship was reported to have crashed in Roswell, New Mexico. Government officials denied the claim. But that was not the truth! We have proof.

Share this article:

Did you find all the clues? Take a look below and see if there were any you missed.

The headline is surprising and not what the article is really about. It is likely clickbait.

The name of the author is not given, so you cannot check who they are.

The site that posted the article is not one you have ever heard of.

https://wownewsnow.net

WOW NEWS NOW

May 4, 2018

ALIENS FOUND ON EARTH!

Reports of real-life aliens living among us.

By Staff Reporter

Want to see real-life aliens? Here is a list of places to travel to see signs that aliens have visited our planet, sponsored by travel.com.

Aliens might have landed on Earth in 1947. A spaceship was reported to have crashed in Roswell, New Mexico. Government officials denied the claim. But that was not the truth! We have proof.

Share this article:

The content says the article was sponsored. The website posted this to make money instead of to inform.

No one was interviewed, and it does not say where the information came from.

It does not say where the image shown came from, so you do not know if it is real.

You Decide!

In some cases, it is totally okay to use material you find online. But other times, copying someone else's content is a big no-no. Read each example below. Then decide whether it falls under fair use. If you need help, reread Chapter 3. When finished, check the answers at the bottom of page 43 to see if you got them right!

1

You use an image from a popular TV show and add a funny caption to make it into a meme.

2

You use another company's logo on a flyer for your babysitting business.

3

You play an entire popular song as background music for an online video.

4

You write online posts that show images of products and give your review of them.

5

You print photos to show as part of a school presentation.

6

You cut out images from magazines to create a collage for an art project.

Answers: 1. It is fair use because the work was used as a joke. 2. Not fair use. You cannot use someone else's work to make money. 3. Not fair use. You used the whole work. 4. It is fair use because you are commenting on the products. 5. It is fair use because it is being used in school for learning purposes. 6. It is fair use because you turned the original work into something new.

True Statistics*

- **Number of new websites added to the internet each day:** 250,000
- **Number of searches Google processes every minute:** 5.9 million
- **Percentage of Americans who say they sometimes get their news from social media:** 54%
- **Number of people worldwide who made at least one edit to Wikipedia in 2023:** 812,635
- **Percentage of Americans who say they see misinformation online daily:** 47%
- **Number of students' assignments partly written by AI, according to Turnitin, an online detection tool:** 1 in 9
- **Number of questions people ask the AI tool ChatGPT each day:** More than 1 billion
- **Number of apps available for download on Google Play and Apple App Store:** 3 million and 1.5 million

* *As of 2024*

Did you find the truth?

FALSE It is never okay to reuse content others have posted online.

TRUE Many apps have features to keep people using them as long as possible.

Resources

Other books in this series:

You can also look at:

Brown, Robin Terry. *Breaking the News: What's Real, What's Not, and Why the Difference Matters*. Washington, D.C.: National Geographic Kids, 2020.

Grant, Joyce. *Can You Believe It?: How to Spot Fake News and Find the Facts*. Toronto: Kids Can Press, 2022.

Graydon, Shari. *Made You Look: How Advertising Works and Why You Should Know*. Toronto: Annick Press, 2013.

Screen Free Heroes: 8 Inspiring Tales of Kids Who Took Back Control, Plus Real Accounts of 8 Legendary Athletes Achieving Greatness Without Digital Distractions. New York: Mysterious Press, 2024.

Glossary

artificial intelligence (ahr-tuh-FISH-uhl in-TEL-i-juhns) the science of making computers do things that previously needed human intelligence, such as understanding language

bias (BYE-uhs) a tendency to favor or oppose something

citing (SITE-ing) crediting the original author or source of information

content (KAHN-tent) text, images, and videos created and posted online

copyright (KAH-pee-rite) the legal right to control the use of something created, such as a song or book

credible (KRED-uh-buhl) believable

digital literacy (DIJ-i-tuhl LIT-ur-uh-see) the ability to find, evaluate, and communicate information using technology

fair use (FAIR YOOS) the law that allows the use of copyrighted material without the author's permission

plagiarism (PLAY-juh-riz-uhm) stealing the ideas or words of another and presenting them as your own

search engine (SURCH EN-jin) a computer program that will search the internet for the words or data you request

Index

Page numbers in **bold** indicate illustrations.

IBD/3 14/1/25

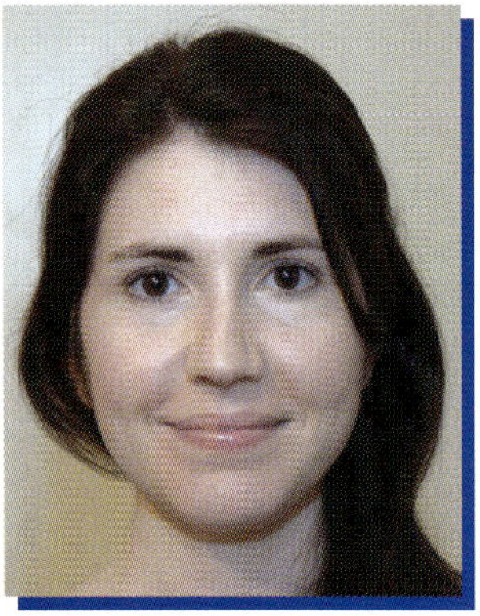

About the Author

Cody Crane is an award-winning nonfiction children's writer. Her favorite subjects to write about are science and art. Special thanks to her ten-year-old son, Eli, who shared his internet knowledge to help her write this book.

Photos ©: cover: jacoblund/Getty Images; back cover: lisegagne/Getty Images; 3: AlexPhotoStock/Alamy Images; 4: CarmenMurillo/Getty Images; 5 bottom right: Devrimb/Getty Images; 6–7: Nikada/Getty Images; 8–9: VioletaStoimenova/Getty Images; 10: Prostock-Studio/Getty Images; 12: IB Photography/Alamy Images; 13: CarmenMurillo/Getty Images; 14 right: Stephen Swintek/Getty Images; 15 center right: tanatat/Getty Images; 16–17: lisegagne/Getty Images; 18: marchmeena29/Getty Images; 19: Mateusz Slodkowski/SOPA Images/LightRocket/Getty Images; 20 left: NetPhotos/Alamy Images; 20 center: digitallife/Alamy Images; 20 right: Mateusz Slodkowski/SOPA Images/LightRocket/Getty Images; 21 center: Devrimb/Getty Images; 22: grinvalds/Getty Images; 26–27 shirts: LiliGraphie/Getty Images; 29: Anastasia Pelikh/Alamy Images; 30: Chesnot/Getty Images; 31: Imgorthand/Getty Images; 32: PeopleImages/Getty Images; 33: Pollyana Ventura/Getty Images; 34–35: monkeybusinessimages/Getty Images; 36: AlexPhotoStock/Alamy Images; 39: Ridofranz/Getty Images; 40, 41 alien: cosmin4000/Getty Images; 40, 41 laptop: Pineapple_Studio; 43 bottom left: Rebecca Emery/Getty Images.

All other photos © Shutterstock.